And Now The Story Lives Inside You

poems by

Elizabeth Reninger

Published by WovenWord Press
811 Mapleton Ave.
Boulder, CO 80304
www.wovenword.com

Cover and book photographs © 2005 by Jenny Morton
Cover and book design © 2005 by Vicki McVey

ISBN: 0971938393
LCCN 2005921598

Contents

III. Trinity   45

for my Teachers

I.
Lao Tzu's Daughter

Harmonics

this morning I add my tracks
to the tracks of deer
each step through snow a silent
word ~ a grace-note finding
its lullaby

in this way we remain mysterious
to each other
even as our walking
through the world makes
a song

we touch in the way stars
touch through their extended
light, or an echo
touches the voice that gave
it wings

I understand very little
and love to meet you
in this way ~ a weaving of
parallel
intentions

mounds of diamonds in dawn's
first Light . . .

Red Rock & Yellow Butterfly

Here on the island
of the immortals
only the most
firm and
subtle survive

blessed and
cursed with my humanity
I hover
somewhere between the stable
regime of geology
and the blissful anarchy
of Spirit

every now and again
grow wings ~ a flow
of ink across
paper ~ gossamer
syllables brushing
rock ~ a vein
of gold remembering

Stardust . . .

Lao Tzu Counsels His Daughter

quivering through marsh-grass thick
with shadow
the gold ribbon
of Bear Creek snakes
silently

falls over
rocks into
a churning froth

then smoothes to a silken
fire again, a bright
mirror, the honeyed
tongue of god, caught between
Earth and Sky

singing its escape
through a field of jade
stalks

Young Buck

covered with the soft
    fur of adolescence
        your antlers are no taller

than your ears
    as in dawn's
        growing light you feed

on tender young
    grasses coming up
        like dreams from the Earth's

revolving sleep
    and bring your shadow with you
        as you walk among the shadows

of trees, every now
    and again glancing up
        into the quiet

beauty of their branches:
    antlers cradling
        pinecones and a spray

of needles framing sky . . .

North Boulder Creek

Here is where the torn
Earth celebrates
where scattered
rock and fallen
trees collaborate
where a wild
tumble of wetness
showers you
with rainbows
Here is where the jagged
rushing creek falls
and falls again
and gathers in quiet
moss-lined pools
her jeweled
surface rippling
Here is where she shatters
her unity and glides
~ a thousand fingers
of quivering light ~
across the rockface before
letting out her silver
hair completely ~
forty feet
of pure
surrender
a galaxy of small
planets thrown
into gravity's
ruthless
freedom . . .

Military Cemetery In Snow

Small white
grave markers shine
rank and file
staunchly linear
as new snow drifts
in bone-chill wind
obliterating some
completely . . .

Bonsai *

Three hundred and ninety-five years ago
pushed my head through Earth's
soft crust
slender as a ray
of light and startled
by a remembered
brightness . . .

sometime later
human hands coaxing
growth in this way and that
mother-to-daughter father-
to-son I've been passed ~ each
a pearl now on the thread
of my survival

I may be small but my vision spans
seven generations
and more ~ I've become a temple
signifying the natural, my needles
a holy script, and this song
in my core still flowing
golden and wild

9
~

as a newborn's . . .

* Shipaku (Chinese Juniper), Shakan (slanting style), 85
cm (34"), 395 years old

Options

the morning sky holds its shifting
continents of clouds
its herd of furry mammals moving
to and fro as they feed
on tender stalks
of light

they touch and merge
and separate, an easy
diplomacy, spontaneous lovemaking as they share this
floating
field of my vision falling

over its illusory
horizons . . .

Weather Vane

And now the body turns
where your breath
     takes it

Wind come down today
from the Flatirons, beyond
that Long's
     Peak

So breathing now the air
of all who've climbed
     there

And flow with Boulder Creek
fresh sound of a whispered
     ancient wisdom

Try to catch your reflected
limbs or face and see:
impossible
     to hold

This dance tells others
where to look, what the weather
     might be

Some say "Yoga" ~
I say what the wind
     says

Winter Creek

fractured light
       sun at noon dances
       scale-like on the surface

while something else beneath
       gurgles through flows
       of ice and snow, fractal

curves a Mendelbrat
       set within this spinning bright
       kaleidoscope of

reflected trees and clouds your
       feet walking are
       its banks its softening

container now
       at noon here in Boulder
       Colorado somewhere

on the surface of
       a shared
       planet gravity from a spinning

bright core what holds
       it together and
       the Tao

           lets it flow . . .

Says Bear Creek

run shallow under the bridge
shiver silver across
    your skin like a rippling

mirror, a quivering
school of minnows, be this widening
    surface that speaks

in patterns reflective
of some unseen geology:
    a bed of rock made fluent

by satin-soft
sheets of water, by terraced layers
    of transparency, slipping in

and out of each other like the bodies
of lovers, bending light to make
    what your mind most deeply

desires: a peacock's wild
plumage, a scattering
    of rainbows, the whispered

    cadence of a poem . . .

Butterfly

thumb-sized
dressed in white
    velvet, flits among

jade spears, a quivering
cathedral of
    leaves, willow and

cottonwood thickening
to green-gold the soft
    banks of boulder creek

as mid-day sun pours through
onto churning
    froth of small

waterfall
shining-white
    white-shining

serene flow surrendering
to ecstasy
    wings of air entering

a riot of
transparency . . .

Likeness

the hummingbird
hovers
as the sun does

just above
ground on the cusp
of dawn

bathed in an ocean
of new
gold her wings

circling
circling at the speed
speed of light before

disappearing
into a forest birthing
shadows

Crossings

after an afternoon
an eternity
of steady rain

with the soft ground still
whispering her
fulfillment

the torn mist bleeding
lapis lazuli, the jewel
of light slowly

emerging ~ this is when
small gatherings of deer
weave their sharp

shyness through
wet trees and shining
rock, when the mystery

of such crossings hold
a magic rich
with possibility ~ your heart

flutters and sings
and this breath you so
commonly call your own

rushes out to join
them in their passage
from the manifest to

the vast and holy unseen . . .

Mother

cradled within the rumble
of in-coming

thunder the raven's
cry becomes

a lullaby . . .

Daybreak

windy sun
at
dawn makes oak

leaves quiver
gold and
shine like the linked

mail the fluid
armor of

a knight . . .

Quarry

here the quiet
forest opens
to flame-red layers
of sandstone

the hooves of deer
crisply cross
its fallen shards

peels of thunder trapped
here like wild
animals might echo
for centuries

as cottonwoods on the ridge
through the storm's first
heavy drops extend

their antlers like silver
lightning, the quarry's
fire growing
brighter and

brighter . . .

Wood Pile

within the silence of dawn I can hear
echoes of an axe-blade
falling

the heartwood lies open now, exposed
with quartered rings showing
maturity

through the bright air this mountain
rises now, saying: Winter
is coming

my years of growing deep
in the forest have brought me
to this ~

this Love at last ready
for burning, within the silence
of dawn I can hear

echoes of a matchstick drawn
across flint, the first
stars ignited

within the mingling of our breath at last
set free, and I can hear
You entering …

Translation

The dappled forest holds the answer
to every unasked question.
Birdsong is the text
you need to decipher.

How deep can you go
into that silence?
Can your bones remember
the spacious quills of feathers?

No lover can match the sweetness
of sap rising to meet
the delicate calligraphy
of a songbird's feet.

Now you've reached the center
of your dream.
You are the coarse
feathers of the scripture

(a robe of bark and pine
needles ~ a parchment
bordering sky)
and its radiant heart

beating, beating . . .

Cress Spring

where Winter willows make a hammock
cradling Winter sky
silver-gray inviting
lapis lazuli

go down to find a frozen
creek softening
where a spring's warm
song comes

flowing in bordered
by green lace, the delicate
wanderings of watercress
and find yourself also

softening there ~ one among a million
young willows held beneath
the ancient one's canopy ~ that fountain
of limbs growing out

of a trunk whose bold circumference
spans the universe ~ imagine
then being
at your own coronation: presented

with anklets of jade
while all around the first
buds of Spring erupt ~ a gilded
crescendo, a ruffled

ecstasy of birdsong …

Morning

Yes ~ I have survived
at least one forest
fire

says the ponderosa, golden
tears dripping
down ashen

bark ...

Photosynthesis

mid-summer.
the mountains in their ten
thousand shades
of green are
resplendent: the trees

thick with emerald dreams;
lime-green meadows
rushing with the wind's
secrets, falling back
to silence;

the creek-rocks soft
with carpets of moss;
shy deer nibbling
tender leaves, leaving
hoof-prints near billowing

mushrooms and ear-
shaped cacti swollen
with last night's rain.
every now
and again a tiny

ladybug appearing
red as the sun's
unseen
center saying:
all it takes is the smallest

intention ~ an ember
of love to set

the whole thing blazing ...

Wolf

elusive as
        a poem, twice this morning
                you crossed my path ~ quick as

refracted light ~ a stroke
        of silver genius ~ a fiercely
                elegant dash

from mystery into
        the manifest ~ pulling the thread
                of my amazed

devotion with you as
        you plunged again
                needle-like through the quivering

skin of the visible
        onto the backside of
                the forest's weave

of trees and rock
        moss and
                softly singing

morning air ...

II.

Consecration

Silhouette

What is this darkness that
in morning breeze ripples
into trees?

That presses to the surface
of my vision like a diver
emerging from the sea?

That with the slowness of
a starry-eyed and shy
toddler or wise sage reveals

its robe of shape and color?
That suddenly I call
my day, my world, my flesh

and bones and marrow ... ?

Basin

this meadow, held in concavity
by a rocky perimeter ~ a rim
from which its grassy
slopes descend, and to which
they return, is where I stand:

an image perched
on the cliff of an eye's
boney orbit, my Love drawn
irresistibly to its center
cast upside-down and backwards

into a larger Intelligence
returned then as an echo
I call my world ~ as a new
form enlivened
enraptured

divinized by
that Surrender …

Deluge

on its loom of gold, its latticework
of lightning, rain pours
from Heaven into your seeing

weeks, months, lifetimes since
last the sky released
such a fury of Truth

if you were the Buddha you could hear
in thunder a universe
of flowers blooming

might even don this wet
surrender as a robe ~ gusts
of wind turning

Love to velvet … might walk right into
that holy fire ~ lakes
of wisdom forming in

the craters left
by your
enormous

steps …

Powa*

First to shine
are the fences.

They catch dawn's curved
light to make their wooden
bodies beautiful.

Behind them breathe
invisible Beings. (If you pause
quietly you can feel them.)

Soon golden branches
will fill the sky. You may wonder:
What is this sadness?
And remember:

That person you thought
you were in last
night's dream hasn't really
died ... She's just

with a pulse of
awakened amber breathing

elsewhere ...

* Powa is a Tibetan Buddhist practice of transferring the
consciousness at the time of death

32
~

Whistle

I walk out into
stars
and clouds
intermingling in the night sky like
ghosts with eyes

Who would be whistling
at this hour?

Overhead the skeletons
of trees loom large
a chilling sight within
this dream I name
as my front yard

Who would be whistling
at this hour?

The snowy owls hunt
for lemmings
bring them back to feed
their young ~ a nest of ivory
fur and yellow moons

Who would be whistling
at this hour?

Now I gaze into the windows
of the house I just
left ~ How strange! to notice
this choice I have: do I
return or not? Who

would be whistling
at this hour?

Sky Burial*

when the blue
wings of dawn
lift lightly out of night's
branched mystery

come to rest on the sloped
backs of mountains and
deer feeding there

then the magpies
make of them a surface
for their own
nourishment ~ they search and find

tiny life burrowing
there in a forest
of fur ~ insects

whose interrupted
lives within this dream
of hooves and beaks suddenly

take flight . . .

* a "sky burial" is a Tibetan Buddhist practice in which
the body of a deceased practitioner is ~ on a mountain-
top ~ ritually dismembered and left as food for scaveng-
ing birds

Migration

gold fire
winter sun a diffuse
ember

flickering flames
flock of geese
escape

shiver-wise to distant
warm paradise

Sakyong Mipham Rinpoche

How stunning is the beauty of silence
          manifest as a man! ~ You in your silks
                    red as molten lava, as the glowing

eyes of a cobra, a thousand blooming
          roses ... What is devotion
                    if not the casual precision

with which you drape a crimson
          robe over your
                    left shoulder? How an easy

sense of humor ~ elegant
          innocent as
                    a thoroughbred ~ bears weighty truths

easily through the gates
          of my heart's deepest
                    hearing ... You

no doubt are none of this
          and more
                    and I the grateful

amazed recipient
          of paradox ~ an image
                    playfully in love

                    with its mirror ...

Dawn

at this time
when the light is not yet
useful, merely
beautiful

when a bright
honey pours
nectar over a curved
horizon, into a nameless

chalice, and your vision
wakes also, as if
to meet it, touching
everything

when for an endless
moment all
colors are
this

color a shimmering
fabric an infinite
wisdom this

body
of pure love, so suddenly

your own ...

Consecration

I am The Great Stupa Of Dharmakaya
That Liberates Upon Seeing.★

I am that sacred
geometry. The equipoise

of Buddha plated
in gold. I am Chakrasamvara

and Vajrayogini ~ their playful
union ... I am The Great Stupa

Of Dharmakaya That Liberates
Upon Seeing. I am the feast

and the liturgy, the clear
and stormy sky. I am the incense

burning ...

★ The Great Stupa Of Dharmakaya That Liberates Upon
Seeing is an architectural tribute to the late Sogyal
Trungpa Rinpoche, and is located at the Shambhala
Mountain Center, Red Feather Lakes, Colorado.

Sand Castles

stroked through morning mist
   all the names
     for yellow gather

as though building from
   scratch their own
     radiant

universe … with time
   unfolding her ten-thousand
     petals the delicate

moments of your life grains
   of sand they give
     ears to every

creature eyes
   that might open ~ hear from
     the distance a golden

     tide rising …

Sunyata

softly as a flock
of angels
crystalline wings alighting

on rock
new snow gathers
whitely on the creek's

shoulders
beneath which flow this braided
tumble of

small waterfalls
the spiraling
mystery of pools

churning up ancient
patterns at their base
as the sky on every

side grows ever
more dense and brightly
open

with a descending
bliss . . .

Leaves

sometimes,
at midday, when
the warm Autumn sky
restless and golden
pours down through
a reckless gentle
rustling of Oak leaves
and that sound
~ you know ~
of some sort
of transition leaves you
with a sadness
hard to pinpoint:
like what exactly
is that shade of blue
that bleeds from dusk
to midnight, appearing
suddenly as darkness
as this vast
illuminated ocean
of stars and galaxies ~
all our hopes
and aspirations now
so clearly visible
and we ~
we gasp at the vision
of such infinite
possibility …

First Snow

Come with me into open space ~ into the meadow
    whose broad shoulders fall away
        softly from Bear Peak. It is before the dawn

of man. You can feel small creatures burrowing
    warmly against the storm. A syntax
        of survival. Silence through and through.

Meanwhile those with roots
    and branches wear the weather
        beautifully ~ are silken in their icy

gowns. Soon the sky's wrinkled
    forehead will smooth. Then they'll shine
        like crystal chandeliers. Become

rivers of light. Then the first
    human will rise
        from her sea of ignorance.

Will remember how to breathe. How to walk as
    though caressing
        the Earth. How to speak in tones the flowers

of snow can hear …

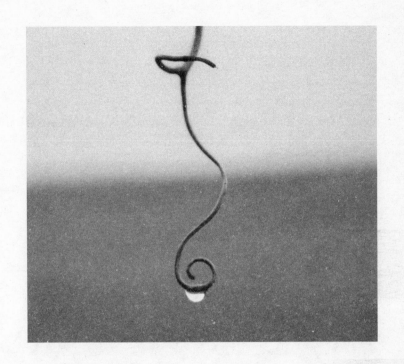

III.
Trinity

Trinity

now one
by one the stars release
their brightness to this dark

mantle of
leaves, to this slow
rising through
abstraction of the quiet

details of
a tree, the textured
torso of

an Oak, the golden
veins of Autumn's
parchment, the feathered
throats invisible

to your eye that signal
the coming of those first
long shadows, a stroked

silence waking
to song, to a flight
of syllables finding
their way into the white

sky of a poem, the deepest
portals of

Your hearing . . .

Shroud Of Turin

now the Winter Earth is wrapped
in downy white, a single
silence marked
here and there by dried
berries, a remembered
passion
the trees are bare

gradually Spring
softens what's beneath, new
leaves emerge from branches
as though from caves

when the first
crocuses push
nail-thin bodies and
opening eyes through
that crystalline cloth you see

in the flush of their startled
beauty your own
True Face slowly

appearing …

Stars Through Winter Oak

Like shadows of remembered
leaves cast onto
heaven, these veins

of light we see as
stars intermingle
lightly with your naked
branches. Inside,

I've set pen to
paper, branched
images made

of ink recreating
a memory ~ that first
time you entered
the dawn of my vision:

a single star wandering
close enough to warm
a frozen Earth.

And now,
every spring the sun
turns green upon my golden
branches …

Stations Of The Cross

like a cross
the quiet
title of this poem

one by one its syllables
becoming flesh

its steps across
ground smooth
and rocky

(is this Kashmir
or Jerusalem?)

at the top of the hill which is the bottom
of this page it will hang
completed

a work of art
a savior

an idea whose halted
breath three
days later will return

emerge as though
resurrected

Continuation

It is the morning
of Christmas eve
Your mind mixes
easily with mist
silver–wet
crystalline ...

A thin moon hovers
somewhere in
the distance ~ a light
snow is the field through
which you leave
your tracks ~ those "lost years"

of Jesus come to mind ~ miles
and miles trekking
the Himalayas ~ cold
and sleet and the beauty
of something growing
rich and
spacious inside ... You return

to your home
in Boulder, Colorado
A white rose in a flurry
of baby's breath
rises from a silver
vase to welcome
You back ...

Hover

Moving their dark forms through the morning air
black ink brushing
a calligraphy of Light
the ravens from their distance draw
beauty into your rising
vision ~ Theirs is a silent
script whose message is as old
as You are: hover here, they say,
in this space between
what you see and what
sees you
Let the warmth of dawn
your Lover's hand fill
the sheen of midnight's
body with new flight
Feel the pull
of the planet whose circling
you circle
Love the sky you're traveling through
Be content to grow
smaller and smaller, leaving only
this curved dome of Heaven as evidence

of your passing ...

Sun Through Storm Clouds

Here is your Love stitching
my wounds to their
primordial Sky

Here is your robe of dawn
wrapping its silky
darkness around Light

Our lovemaking spills
rainbows from
its ecstasy ~

a palette of
joyful play, a mutual
awakening

While in the field nearby
Krishna brings to soft
lips a flute, opens

your ears with
the golden
thread of his song, your own

voice at last emerging …

Crescent Moon, Morning Star

such purity afloat
beneath your risen lids!

A fullness carved out
by sky. A lithe

bow drawn taut
now on the pulsing string

of your mind. God's first
finger supporting this

invisible arrow
whose shining tip

is the morning star, finding
its target in the spacious

core of your heart ...

Juniper

a communion wafer becoming
thin on the pink
tongue of dawn

a Winter Solstice full
moon opens
your vision as she
slowly disappears ...

now the low
lying juniper presents you
with his galaxy of
jewels ~ blue

berries arranged
to reflect the whole
universe

each draws the deepening
sky into its orbit
sits quietly content
as a Buddha

brewing in her gentle
smile the sweetly
intoxicating flavor

of Heaven ...

Winter Birch & Stars

branching to infinity
your light is a boundless
celebration
holds within its rapture a thousand
galaxies

naked beneath every
heaven you compose
a melody so fine only
children and
angels can hear it

as when a rising
receding tide whispers
its secrets to miles
miles of white sand ~ each
grain a phrase

or syllable awakened
and you who've walked
this beach forever ~
where your footprints used to be now
a reflected moon ~ now your own

voice singing ...

Composition

all Winter long
the shining silver trees hold
this condensation of
color ~ a palette
of dried berries

all Winter long you walk
beneath and through and around
those limbs, wondering: what vivid
life lies tightly
tucked within?

all Winter a relentless
sky moves through its kaleidoscope
of refracted Light ~ a Love
in turns harsh
and gentle

all Winter long some quiet
melody yearns
for expression, begins to grow
flesh upon the stark
blueprint of
its bones

And now it's Spring ...

Leaves On Snow

As the memory of yesterday's storm
fills slowly with
golden warmth

the white ocean recedes, leaving
a shore of leaves
a scattering of veined

sea shells whispering
to soft
flesh the lost

secrets of trees ...

The Poet

parallel in Spring snow
silver air quivers

as pine boughs grow
heavy with crystalline
kisses ...

nearby the creek
roars, tumbling down from
invisible mountains

while here in my garden
quiet red
tulips offer their soft

lips their opening
mouths to the falling
sky to a shattered

silence like
chalices ...

White Water

last night snow and now
   all along her banks the Spring
      trees heavy with

blossoms giving off scent
   to crystalline air
      last night snow and a shower

of starlight coming down later
   to mingle with her flowering
      currents

last night the heavy
   boughs of darkness
      breath by whispered

breath awakened
   and now the golden
      footsteps of

lovers long
   gone slowly
      melting, the brimming

creek silent as ever ...

Spring Storm

now a gust
of blossoms takes you
there

a spiral dance
dervishes in
white skirts

while naked trees raise
their arms to an indifferent
sky

to passion rolling
over the mountains
to a gold

thread whose endless
clarity breaks
open their hearts

forever …

61
~

Clouds

serene
silent
aloof

in their white robes the clouds
define the curved
purity, the ephemeral
grace of heaven

descend one day as a flock
of angels, a white
fire of
blossoms, the sweetest

fragrance flowing out from
your limbs as you sit
humble and
amazed as
a gopi at the feet
of her Beloved

the deep roots of Spring's
awakening ...

Birches

in Winter the white-skinned
   birches become
      spidery webs ~ matrices

of Light capturing
   blue sky …
      grow up from

frozen ground to hold
   your vision there
      where songbirds sailing

in from
   the invisible greet a quiet
      dawn ~ tethering the secret

pulse of stars
   to a melody your human
      brightness can

hear ~ your quivering
   limbs receive
      easily as a flock

      of small birds …

Branches

about the size
of an Oak leaf
translucent in

dawn's golden
breeze
the crescent

moon hovers
near Venus in blue
branches

as a flock of small
birds lift
from song into

silence
leaving you
there standing

empty as
an echo
a slowly

dissolving planet ...

Labyrinth

on the ground-floor of the First
Methodist Church, half-sunken
into Earth

is a labyrinth, a symmetrical
swirl, some sweet forest,
beckoning ...

Go there to find
her perimeter of candles
flickering blue in opaque
votives, golden
halos dancing ...

Walk slowly her intricate
maze, that sacred
geometry, the petals
of a flower whose tender
mystery leads

at last to this: some tiny
flame upon its golden
stem ~ wicking up

a sweetness un-
imagined ~ your own

fragrant Center ...

Crescent Moon

At this time,
with the sky's black satin
wrinkled with a million
stars

a golden scythe
a curved sword rests
expectant in its circular
casing, its sheath
of sky

and all the constellations
of your mind ~ heroes
monsters and
saints ~ spin out their shining
epics, their weave
of war and salvation

all this upon the trembling
surface of your
eyes ~ a pair
of moons dancing
together through their sensual
orbit

so now the story lives
inside you ~ a hologram of
completeness, a beautiful
dream ~ as you draw
that sword and enter
fearlessly into dawn's

approaching Light ...

Late Autumn

as if drawing his
lost leaves back
up to naked
branches

the maple's quiet
silhouette pulls orange
silk from a waking
horizon

pauses here
with you on the cusp
of dawn then with a single
cardinal bursts

into a fire of song . . .

Turning

Now the last stars beckon
from this dream of a world's
slow waking, a waking slow
as some light remembering
your body or your body
remembering that light

Cast your glance deeply
to the West at dusk
to find it flowing
back to you on tender
wings of gold next morning

We are that turning
whose dream divides
dusk from dawn, whose waking
mends a fractured vision
Now gaze into the eyes

of your Lover ~ that distant
star whose Light has traveled
lifetimes now to touch
your human
skin … Revel in that warm

eternity … !

MoonBath

never before has darkness held
such tender possibility ...

never before has your collusion with
the infinite produced

such quiet vast
illumination ...

never before has your embrace
satisfied me so

completely ...

BirdBath

only this
matters: this ecstatic
baptism

this standing on stick-
thin legs where the singing
creek pools at the lip
of the waterfall

only this
ruby-feathered
chest diving to meet
its reflection

this beak piercing
again and again that quivering
surface, these wings half-
unfolding, a ruffle

of joy guiding rivers
of light a tumble
of droplets dressed
in rainbows along your hidden
spine

shattering all
decorum beneath
blue branches in quiet

assent ...